DUSTED AND BUSTED!

The Science of Fingerprinting

D.B. Beres

WARNING: All of the cases in this book are true. At least one of them involves a **BLOODY FINGERPRINT** left behind at the scene of a murder.

Franklin Watts®
A Division of Scholastic Inc.
New York • Toronto • London • Auckland • Sydney
Mexico City • New Delhi • Hong Kong
Danbury, Connecticut

CONTENTS

TRUE OR FALSE?

This glue can
help you see
invisible
fingerprints!

SUPER GLUE

NET WT. 2g

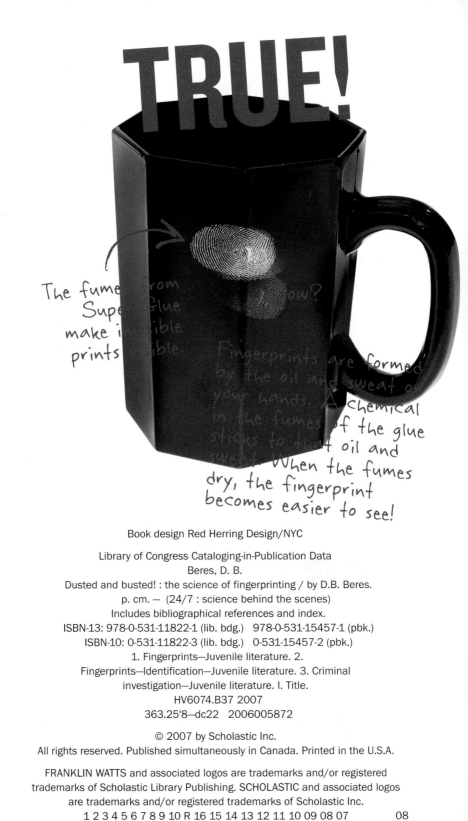

TRUE!

The fumes from Super Glue make invisible prints visible.

How?

Fingerprints are formed by the oil and sweat on your hands. A chemical in the fumes of the glue sticks to that oil and sweat. When the fumes dry, the fingerprint becomes easier to see!

Book design Red Herring Design/NYC

Library of Congress Cataloging-in-Publication Data
Beres, D. B.
Dusted and busted! : the science of fingerprinting / by D.B. Beres.
p. cm. — (24/7 : science behind the scenes)
Includes bibliographical references and index.
ISBN-13: 978-0-531-11822-1 (lib. bdg.)   978-0-531-15457-1 (pbk.)
ISBN-10: 0-531-11822-3 (lib. bdg.)   0-531-15457-2 (pbk.)
1. Fingerprints—Juvenile literature. 2.
Fingerprints—Identification—Juvenile literature. 3. Criminal
investigation—Juvenile literature. I. Title.
HV6074.B37 2007
363.25'8—dc22   2006005872

1 2 3 4 5 6 7 8 9 10 R 16 15 14 13 12 11 10 09 08 07   08

PERFUME

In Chattanooga, a thief robs a local drugstore.

These cases are 100% real. Find out how fingerprint analysts solved a handful of mysteries.

15 Case #1:
The Burglar with No Prints

A burglar robs a store and appears to leave no prints behind. How does the fingerprint expert make the ID?

25 Case #2:
The Duffel Bag Murder

A gruesome crime has been committed. Can fingerprint evidence help nail the criminal?

Hikers in Tennessee get an awful shock.

35 Case #3:
The Barefoot Bandit

Can a burglar be identified from his footprint?

In Paris, TN, a thief makes a major misstep.

FORENSIC DOWNLOAD

Here's even more amazing stuff about fingerprinting—right here at your fingertips.

YELLOW PAGES

You probably already know that your fingerprints are unique. That's what makes them a great method of identification.

FORENSIC 411

Say there's been a robbery. Police arrive on the scene. One of the first things they'll do is search for fingerprints. If the thief has left a fingerprint, that could lead to a quick arrest.

IN THIS SECTION:

▶ how fingerprint analysts REALLY TALK;

▶ how good you are at MATCHING FINGERPRINTS;

▶ who usually shows up to process CRIME SCENES.

Dusted and Busted

Stop! Before you get your prints all over this book, learn the vocabulary of fingerprint analysts.

"Look, I know you think of me as just a fingerprint specialist. But I prefer to call myself an expert in dactylography."

specialist
(SPEH-shul-ist) someone who knows a lot about something

dactylography
(dac-ti-LOG-rah-fee) the study of fingerprints as a method of identification

"Dactylo" means "having to do with fingers or toes." "Graphy" means "the study of."

"Check out the ridges in these fingerprints. They form a pattern that looks like a little tornado!"

ridges
(RI-jez) raised lines on the tips of your fingers that create your fingerprint. The area between the ridges is called a groove.

fingerprints
(FIN-ger-prints) the pattern of skin ridges at the tips of your fingers. These patterns include arches, loops, and whorls.

"Nope, the fingerprints don't match. We're going to have to let the suspect go."

Say What?

> "I want someone to dust the whole car! There must be *some* latent prints in there!"

latent prints
(LAY-tuhnt prints) finger-prints or footprints that you can't see. When people touch stuff, the oils on their skin leave a mark. That means that every time you touch a hard, shiny surface, you're leaving an invisible fingerprint!

> "I'm sure we didn't miss a spot, sir. We dusted for prints everywhere."

dusted
(DUS-ted) brushed a dark fingerprint powder on a surface as you're looking for latent prints. The dust sticks to the sweat and oils in the latent prints. That makes invisible prints visible!

Here's other lingo fingerprint specialists might use on the job.

prints
(prints) short for *fingerprints*
"We found **prints** all over the soda bottle."

busted
(BUS-tid) caught; found out
"We **busted** that crook!"

partial
(PAR-shul) part of a fingerprint. It's short for *partial fingerprint*.
"Hey, did anyone notice this **partial** on the door?"

perp
(purp) people who have committed crimes. It's short for *perpetrator*.
"The **perp** is now in jail."

process
(PRAH-ses) to gather information (such as fingerprint evidence) at a crime scene
"Get some experts to **process** the scene!"

Partials

Which Matches?

Instructions: Look at each partial fingerprint on the left. Then choose the matching fingerprint from the four to the right.

Evidence at Hand

You leave a mark almost everywhere you go.

Take a look at the ends of your fingers. You'll see small ridges made of skin. The ridges have a purpose. They help you get a better grip on stuff you pick up.

These ridges form patterns called fingerprints. Your fingerprints were formed even before you were born. They never change. And no one has fingerprints just like yours. That's why fingerprinting is such a good way of **identifying** someone.

There are several kinds of fingerprints. Here are the terms the specialists use.

▶ **latent prints:** They're formed when you touch something and the oil or sweat on your hand leaves a print. Latent prints are mostly invisible to the naked eye. Fingerprinting dust makes them visible.

▶ **patent prints:** These are clearly visible. They're made when you touch something like paint or blood and then touch other surfaces.

▶ **impressed prints:** These are made when you touch something like gum that leaves a clear impression of your prints.

▶ **partial prints:** Partials are incomplete prints.

The Forensic Team

Fingerprint specialists work as part of a team to help solve crimes and identify victims.

FORENSIC DNA SPECIALISTS

They collect DNA from blood or body fluids left at the scene. Then they use this evidence to identify victims and suspects.

CRIME SCENE INVESTIGATORS

They study the scene of a crime and process evidence. They often have to speak in court about what they found.

DETECTIVES OR AGENTS

They direct the crime investigation. They collect information about the crime, interview witnesses, identify suspects—and arrest them if there's enough evidence!

TRACE EVIDENCE SPECIALISTS

They collect trace evidence at the scene. That includes fibers, tire tracks, shoe prints, and more. Can this evidence lead them to a criminal?

FINGERPRINT SPECIALISTS

They find, photograph, and collect fingerprints at the scene. Then they compare them to prints they have on record.

MEDICAL EXAMINERS

They're medical doctors who investigate suspicious deaths. They try to find out when and how someone died. They often direct other members of the team.

24 hours a day, 7 days a week, 365 days a year, fingerprint specialists are solving mysteries.

IN THIS SECTION:

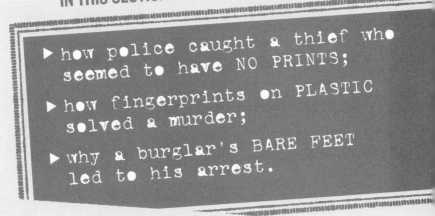

- ▶ how police caught a thief who seemed to have NO PRINTS;
- ▶ how fingerprints on PLASTIC solved a murder;
- ▶ why a burglar's BARE FEET led to his arrest.

Note: These three case files are true. However, names, places, and other details have been changed. In addition, the photos in these stories are to give you a picture of what happened. They are not from these crimes.

Here's how fingerprint analysts get the job done.

What does it take to solve a crime? Good fingerprint analysts don't just make guesses. They're like scientists. They follow a step-by-step process.

As you read the case studies, you can follow along with them. Keep an eye out for the icons below. They'll clue you in to each step along the way.

At the beginning of a case, fingerprint analysts **identify one or two main questions** they have to answer.

The next step is to **gather and analyze evidence**. Fingerprint analysts collect as much information as they can. Then they study it to figure out what it means.

When they've studied all the data, fingerprint analysts **come to a conclusion**. Where are the fingerprints? And who left them? If they can answer those questions, they may have cracked the case.

Chattanooga, Tennessee
October 15, 2005, 9:15 A.M.

The Burglar with No Prints

A burglar robs a store and appears to leave no prints behind. How does the fingerprint expert make the ID?

15

Escape Artist

A thief drops in on a drugstore and leaves the scene without a trace.

Bob Moranes had a terrible surprise when he arrived at work on October 15.

Mr. Moranes was the owner of Gooch Pharmacy near Chattanooga, Tennessee. That morning, when he walked to the back of his drugstore, his heart jumped. Everything was a mess. Items from the shelves lay on the floor. Bottles were missing. The cash register was open—and empty.

Moranes called the police. As he waited for them to arrive, he went through the mess. A lot of medicine was missing.

Then he checked to see how the burglar had entered the store. The back door and the windows were locked from the inside. How had the burglar gotten in? And where had he or she gone?

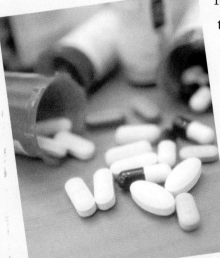

When the owner of Gooch Pharmacy arrived, his drugstore was a mess.

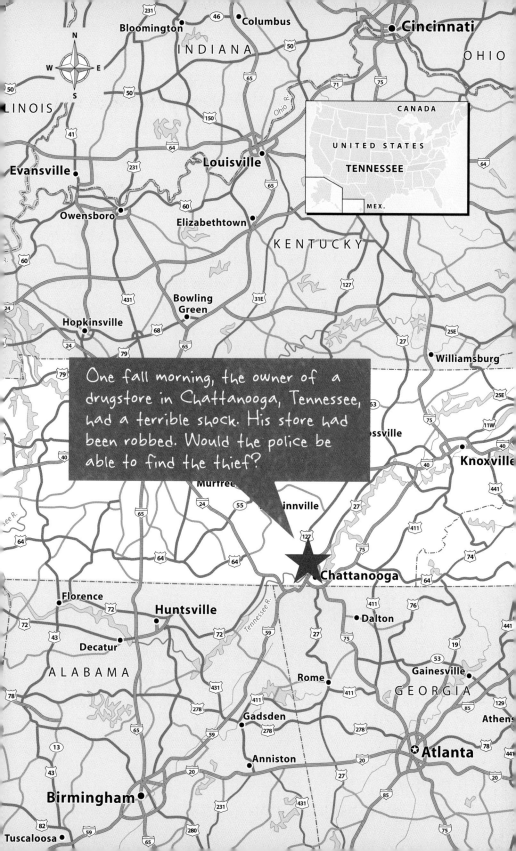

One fall morning, the owner of a drugstore in Chattanooga, Tennessee, had a terrible shock. His store had been robbed. Would the police be able to find the thief?

Scoping the Scene

Investigators look for clues to the thief's escape.

Soon the police arrived. They wanted to figure out how the thief had gotten inside.

They found a clue in a back office. The cover to a heating **duct** in the ceiling had been removed. Ducts are the passages that allow air to move around in a building.

That's not all. In the office, a desk had been moved directly under the opening to the duct.

Where did that duct lead? The police traced it to the heating system on the roof. They found an opening next to it.

After the burglary, investigators dusted drawers and other surfaces for prints.

Now the police had a theory about how the burglar entered and left the store. He climbed into the opening on the roof. He crawled through the ducts. Then he kicked out the duct cover and dropped to the floor.

When the burglar was ready to leave, he dragged the desk across the floor. He placed it under the hole in the ceiling. He climbed onto the desk and then pulled himself through the hole.

But who was this guy?

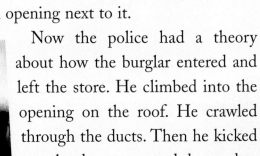

THE MAN WITH NO FINGERPRINTS

This guy was *really* determined not to leave any prints behind.

Robert James Pitts had a long history of arrests. He was tired of getting caught. In 1941 he thought of a plan. He hoped it would keep him out of jail forever.

Pitts found a doctor who was willing to perform a strange operation. The doctor removed the top layers of skin on Pitts's fingertips. Then he tried to replace it with skin from Pitts's chest.

This plan was only partly successful.

A suspect is arrested. Even without fingerprints, that's the situation Robert James Pitts found himself in many times.

Pitts didn't have any fingerprints. But the skin from his chest didn't grow on his fingertips. Pitts was left with thick scar tissue on his fingers. He had no ridges or sense of touch.

And the operation didn't keep Pitts out of jail, either. About a year later, he was arrested. Police were surprised to find that their suspect had no fingerprints.

But they took prints of the middle sections of each of his fingers. They compared the prints to files from the **FBI**, and Pitts was identified.

The Search for Clues

Investigators find no prints inside—but what about outside?

THE EVIDENCE

The fingerprint team arrived at the store to process the scene.

Burglars often leave prints where they enter and exit a crime scene. The investigators knew how the burglar broke into the store. So that's where the print team started. They dusted the heating system and the duct cover.

But they didn't find any prints.

They dusted the cash register. No prints.

They dusted all the boxes and bottles of medicine that were out of place. No prints.

The only clue was a few pieces of black tape. An officer had been sent to figure out how the burglar had gotten off the roof. The officer found a ladder in the back of the building.

Next to the ladder, the officer found several pieces of black tape. He picked one up and noticed a print pressed into the sticky stuff on the tape. He carefully bagged the tape as **evidence**. He sent it to the crime lab.

Would the tape help the police catch the burglar? Or would this be another dead end?

One police officer found some clues outside the drugstore. There were seven or eight wads of black tape like this one.

EVIDENCE

DON'T FORGET TO DUST

How do fingerprint analysts collect and analyze the evidence?

Photographing the Scene

Fingerprint **analysts** first make sure the crime scene has been photographed. That way, there's a record of what the scene looked like right after the crime.

Dusting for Prints

▶ Then the specialists start to process the scene.

▶ They use a dark powder that sticks to the oil and sweat in fingerprints. That makes the fingerprints more visible.

▶ They dust anything the perp might have touched—like doors, walls, counters, and furniture.

▶ They take small stuff like weapons or tools back to the lab. They'll check those for prints, too.

Lifting the Prints

▶ When specialists find a print, they use something sticky, like tape, to **lift** the print. They may also photograph the print to scan into the computer.

▶ They stick the tape to a card and write where and when it was lifted.

▶ Back at the lab, fingerprint specialists process all the small items for prints.

Finding a Perp

▶ If they find a good print, fingerprint specialists compare it to prints from **suspects**.

▶ Or print specialists may run the print through **AFIS**. That's a computer **database** with millions of prints.

For more about AFIS, go to page 23.

Analysts dust fingerprint powder on a counter to reveal a fingerprint.

A Trace of Evidence

Could a few pieces of tape help catch a criminal?

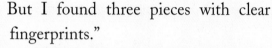

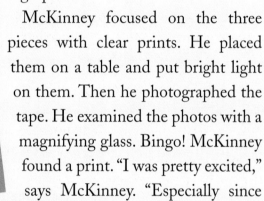

Back at the crime lab, fingerprint specialist Oakley McKinney examined the bits of tape. "There were seven or eight pieces of tape," he says. "Some were wadded up or smashed. But I found three pieces with clear fingerprints."

McKinney focused on the three pieces with clear prints. He placed them on a table and put bright light on them. Then he photographed the tape. He examined the photos with a magnifying glass. Bingo! McKinney found a print. "I was pretty excited," says McKinney. "Especially since there were no other prints at the scene. This could be the evidence the police needed to make an arrest."

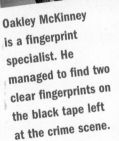

Oakley McKinney is a fingerprint specialist. He managed to find two clear fingerprints on the black tape left at the crime scene.

McKinney scanned the photos of the fingerprints into the AFIS computer system. That's a computer database with thousands of fingerprints.

Would AFIS give the police a lucky break?

FINGERPRINTS GO DIGITAL

A computer database called AFIS makes fingerprint searches faster and more thorough.

Say you're a fingerprint specialist. You go to a crime scene and manage to find some great fingerprints. You lift the prints. Then you go back to the police station. There, you have to look through thousands of prints to find a match.

Wouldn't it be great if there were an easier way?

In fact there is. It's called AFIS. That stands for Automated Fingerprint Identification System. (Print specialists say it like a name—AY-fiss.)

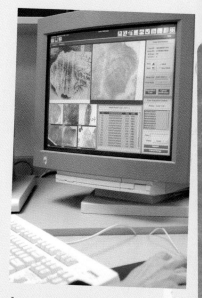

A Database of Fingerprints

AFIS is a computer database where police can store the prints of arrested suspects. Fingerprint specialists can enter prints they've found at crime scenes into AFIS. The computer then does a search. If it finds a match, the specialist checks to make sure AFIS is right.

In 1999, the FBI made this system even more efficient. It created IAFIS. The "I" stands for *integrated*, which means "joined together." IAFIS has joined together AFIS systems from all over the country. Now fingerprint specialists can compare prints they find to millions of prints from all over the U.S.

A computer screen with the results of an AFIS search.

Trapped by the Tape!

Police ID the suspect. But can they find him?

THE CONCLUSION

AFIS compared the prints McKinney had found to millions of prints on file. It came up with a match. McKinney double-checked the computer's results. It was a **hit!** "The suspect's name was Jeffrey Snyder," says McKinney. "He lived north of town. He had a prior arrest for burglary."

The police went to Snyder's home. And Snyder tried to make another sneaky escape—out the back window! Officers tackled him in his backyard. Inside Snyder's house, they found some of the medicines from Gooch Pharmacy.

Snyder eventually confessed that he'd stolen money and medicine from the store. He'd taped the ends of his fingers to make sure he wouldn't leave any fingerprints. But he removed the tape behind the store. He didn't realize that his fingerprints were stuck to the tape.

That mistake made the burglary charges stick! 24/7

Using the fingerprints found on the tape, police tracked down the thief. Not long after, Jeffrey Snyder was arrested.

In the next case, find out how fingerprint evidence helped investigators bag a brutal criminal.

Crossville, Tennessee
July 15, 2000
8:20 A.M.

The Duffel Bag Murder

**A gruesome crime has been committed.
Can fingerprint evidence help
nail the criminal?**

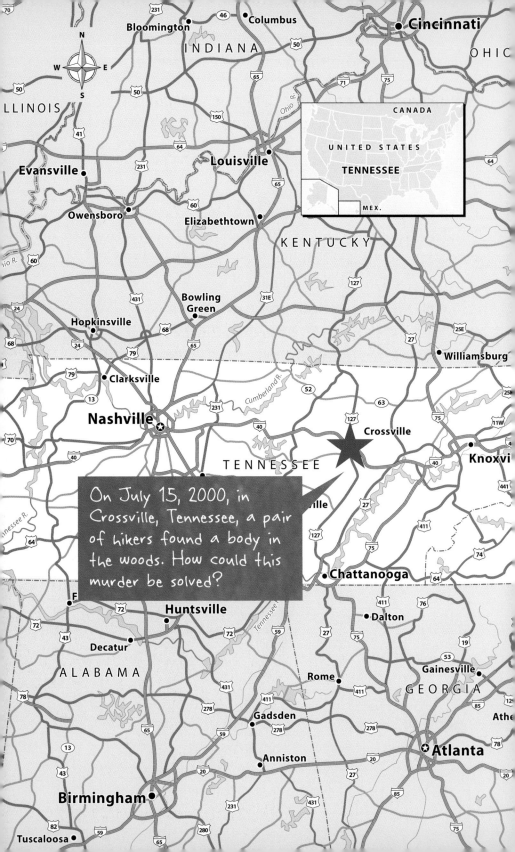

On July 15, 2000, in Crossville, Tennessee, a pair of hikers found a body in the woods. How could this murder be solved?

Trail of Terror

Two hikers are out for a nice day in the woods. Then they make a bloody discovery.

Ryan and Heather Chase loved hiking the wooded trails in Tennessee. On July 15, they were exploring an old logging road. They noticed a faded duffel bag in a ditch. Ryan unzipped the bag. Then he jumped back. "There's a body in there!" he gasped.

When the sheriff and deputies arrived, they examined the bag. They found what they thought were human body parts. They searched the scene and found several more duffel bags.

This case was big. The sheriff was going to need expert help. He called the Tennessee Bureau of Investigation (TBI).

The sheriff and his deputies found duffel bags like this one in the Tennessee woods.

Bagging the Evidence

The TBI looks for clues at the scene.

Agent Todd Dawson from the TBI arrived on the scene. He was leading the investigation.

Dawson knew he had to answer two main questions. Who was the victim? And who was the killer?

Dawson directed his agents to search the area for clues.

Agents found five large duffel bags. Each contained body parts. It looked like all the parts belonged to one body. But Dawson wasn't sure yet.

The agents checked the area where each bag was found. They looked for blood and other **trace evidence** that might have come from the killer.

Investigators found five large duffel bags in a wooded area.

The duffel bags themselves were bloody inside. However, there was no blood in the area around the bags. That suggested that the body had been cut up somewhere else.

That was one clue. To find others, Agent Dawson knew that he'd need help from **experts**. He and his deputies carefully gathered the evidence.

A Close Look at the Victim

Did the body hold any clues to the murder?

Agent Dawson and his deputies brought the evidence back to the TBI crime lab.

The body parts were removed from the duffel bags. They were sent to the office of Dr. Ralph Roberts, the medical examiner. Medical examiners are doctors in charge of investigating suspicious deaths.

Dr. Roberts would try to identify the victim. He'd also try to figure out how the victim was killed.

The victim's body parts had been wrapped in plastic before being stuffed into the duffels. Dr. Roberts unwrapped each body part.

Dr. Roberts concluded that the parts belonged to a single victim. It was a young white male. And he'd been killed by a gunshot wound to the head.

Dr. Roberts still needed to identify the victim. He called in fingerprint expert Oakley McKinney.

McKinney inked the victim's fingers and pressed them to print cards.

Then he took the victim's fingerprints and scanned them into AFIS.

To see a fingerprint ID card, go to page 50.

29

THE CONCLUSION

McKinney got a break! AFIS matched the prints with 29-year-old Dale Givens.

Now that the victim had a name, Dawson began interviewing Givens's friends and family. He hoped one of them had information that might lead him to the killer. But the key piece of evidence was yet to come.

Examining the Evidence

Investigators examine the duffel bags. Were there clues?

For more information about AFIS, see page 23.

Meanwhile, back at the crime lab, **forensics** experts examined the duffel bags.

Trace specialists looked carefully for evidence. Traces of hair or clothing fibers could give them more information about the victim or the killer. But they couldn't find anything useful.

DNA specialists then took samples of the blood. DNA is like a fingerprint. No two people have the same DNA. The specialists hoped to find the killer's DNA. That could help investigators track him down. But they

McKinney thought he had found a bloody thumbprint. But the print came from a toe.

were disappointed. All the blood came from the victim.

Then Dawson noticed something on a piece of plastic that had been wrapped around a body part. It looked like a bloody footprint.

He sent the plastic to fingerprint specialist McKinney for processing. McKinney found several prints. "I found what I thought was a thumbprint," he said. "But it turned out to be the print from a big toe."

TBI's database didn't contain footprints. So the toe print was no help. Was the investigation stalled?

PRINT PROCESSING PRIMER

Fingerprint specialists process fingerprints in different ways. Here's a look at how different prints are handled.

Type of Evidence: fingerprints on hard surfaces such as glass, plastic, or metal
Method: dusting or Super Glue **fuming**

Type of Evidence: fingerprints on soft, **absorbent** surfaces such as paper, cardboard, or unfinished wood
Method: use a chemical called **Ninhydrin**, or send to lab

Type of Evidence: bloody prints
Method: photograph, then send to lab

Type of Evidence: wet prints
Method: allow to dry, then photograph

Printed!

Will the search for a bloody fingerprint finally pay off?

McKinney refused to give up. If he found just one fingerprint, he might be able to solve the case.

McKinney went back to the bloody plastic. He found more prints. But they turned out to be from toes, too. He found a few that looked like fingerprints. But they were smeared or damaged.

McKinney had another idea. Was it possible that there were latent prints on the plastic? Latent prints are fingerprints that are invisible to the eye.

McKinney decided to try a process called fuming, which makes latent prints visible. First, he cut the plastic into smaller sheets. Then he put them inside a special chamber.

Fumes from heated Super Glue were released into the chamber. These fumes make invisible prints visible.

When McKinney took the sheets out of the chamber, he examined them carefully with a magnifying glass. There it was: a fingerprint.

THE EVIDENCE

Fuming makes invisible prints visible. The fumes from Super Glue stick to the chemicals in sweat and oil that form fingerprints. When the fumes are dry, the fingerprints turn white.

McKinney photographed the print and entered it into AFIS. He got a hit. The print belonged to a man named Joseph Parks.

THE CONCLUSION

"AFIS told us it was a print from a left ring finger," McKinney said.

McKinney called Agent Dawson. "I told him we had a match on the plastic print. I gave him the suspect's name." McKinney was confident he had found the killer. "When you find a fingerprint wrapped up with body parts, you can be pretty sure it's the perpetrator's," he said.

A LASTING IMPRINT

How long will a fingerprint stay at the scene of the crime?

A fingerprint can disappear immediately. Or it can last forever. It depends on where the print is and what made it, says specialist Oakley McKinney. Here's a look at some of the factors that affect the quality of a fingerprint.

Dirty hands make good prints.
If the print is made with clean hands, it's usually pretty faint. If the hands are dirty, the prints are usually better. And if the person had paint, blood, or ink on their hands, those prints will last a long time.

Fingerprints stick best to hard, smooth surfaces.
Fingerprint specialists can lift fingerprints off soft, absorbent surfaces like paper or clothing. But fingerprints left on glass or other hard, smooth surfaces last longer.

Don't leave prints out in the rain.
Sun, wind, rain, and cold can damage prints.

Bagged!

A single fingerprint brings the murderer to justice.

Investigators tracked Joseph Parks to Nashville, Tennessee. Police searched Parks's apartment. He had tried to scrub his place clean. But investigators still found trace evidence that linked him to the victim.

Parks was arrested. McKinney's toe print evidence came in handy. Parks's footprints matched those on the bloody plastic!

Police also questioned Parks's girlfriend. She told them that Givens had come to Parks's apartment for a drug deal. The deal went bad, and Parks killed Givens.

Eventually, the case went to court. The prosecutor showed the fingerprint that McKinney had found on the plastic. He explained that AFIS had traced the print to Joseph Parks.

Together with other evidence, the fingerprint convinced the **jury**. Parks was found guilty of murder. He is serving a life sentence. 24/7

The latent fingerprint and the bloody toe print from the plastic helped prove that Parks was guilty.

Find out how evidence from a criminal's feet also played a role in the next investigation.

Paris, Tennessee
September 7, 1979
5:12 A.M.

The Barefoot Bandit

Can a burglar be identified from his footprint?

Burger Break-In

A thief steals some money—and leaves a trail of footprints behind.

It was a beautiful morning when Tim McCall arrived early for work. McCall was the assistant manager of the Burger Queen in Paris, Tennessee. So he was often the first person to get to work.

As usual, McCall began to get the restaurant ready to open. It seemed like a normal day.

But then McCall noticed that the office door was open. He walked in and saw papers on the floor. The window above the desk was open. There were black footprints across the

In Paris, Tennessee, a burglar broke in to the local Burger Queen. The only evidence left behind were some footprints. Could the Tennessee Bureau of Investigation solve this one?

Mississippi 62

Julian M. Carrol.

KENTUCKY

641 68

the Lakes

Lake Barclay 24

Fort Donelson 79

45E

Paris

Kentucky Lake

79

79

45W

Jackson

45

CANADA

UNITED STATES

TENNESSEE

MEX.

65

N
W E

room to the door. Strangely, they were from bare feet!

McCall quickly checked the cash box. It was kept in a desk drawer. It usually contained about $100 in change. The drawer had been pried open. And the cash box was missing.

It was time to call the police.

When the assistant manager arrived at Burger Queen, he found that the office had been broken into.

Looking for Clues

Investigators found no trace of fingers, but plenty of toes.

When the police arrived, McCall showed them the crime scene.

The police investigators had one main goal. It was to figure out the identity of the burglar.

They immediately began processing the scene for fingerprints and other clues.

Fingerprint specialists always look for prints where the criminals enter and exit the crime scene. At the Burger Queen, the window had been forced open. That's probably how the burglar had come in. So the officers

Fingerprint analysts always look for prints where criminals enter and exit the scene. Here, an analyst dusts for prints on a door.

THE EVIDENCE

dusted around the window and door. One officer checked outside the window for evidence.

They also dusted the handles of the desk drawers. Another officer gathered things the burglar might have touched. He carefully took items from the desk drawers and put them in bags. Later, he'd take them to the print lab to be checked for fingerprints.

But the search didn't turn up any fingerprints. This burglar must have been wearing gloves.

There was just one more piece of evidence—the prints from the bare feet.

The investigators had an idea where the prints came from. They thought the burglar had opened the window and climbed onto the desk. Then he had stepped on a piece of **carbon paper** on the desk. Carbon paper is covered with fine, black dust. The black dust must have stuck to the burglar's feet.

The thief stepped on carbon paper, which is covered with black dust. He then walked across the floor.

Carbon paper was used before there were computers. Typists used carbon paper to make copies. They placed a sheet of carbon paper between two sheets of white paper.

The burglar then jumped to the floor and walked across the room. As he did, he left perfect black footprints.

Police photographed the footprints on the floor. They couldn't enter the prints into a database like AFIS. But who knew? Maybe the photos of the footprints would come in handy later.

PRINT PRIVACY
Can the police look at your prints?

What if you're suspected of a crime? Can the police make you give them your fingerprints or footprints?

If you've been arrested, the answer is yes. Police are allowed to take suspects' fingerprints or footprints without their permission. But if you haven't been arrested, the answer is no. Police must get your permission before they take a fingerprint or footprint.

IF THE SHOE FITS

What can police tell from a pair of shoe prints?

Burglars rarely steal in their bare feet. A perp's shoe prints are sometimes left in dirt, mud, or snow at the scene of a crime. In that case, trace evidence experts will process the prints. They photograph them to study later.

Shoeprints can tell the police a lot. If the prints are deep, that could mean that the suspect is heavy. If the footprints are far apart, the person may have been running.

The pattern on the bottom of the shoe can also be a clue. Investigators may be able to tell what kind of shoe the suspect was wearing.

Investigators might also take samples of dirt from the crime scene. When police have a suspect, they'll test the dirt on his shoes. Is there a match?

Following the Trail

**Police have a print from the Barefoot Bandit.
Now they need a foot to match.**

The footprint was pretty good evidence. In fact, toe prints are like fingerprints. Each person's toe prints are unique.

Still, they needed a suspect.

The police had a few leads. They wanted to question Burger Queen employees. They also wanted to talk to past employees.

In addition, they planned to question local people who had been arrested before for burglary. The Burger Queen burglar had known not to leave fingerprints. So maybe this person had stolen before.

The police began their investigation by talking with people who had arrest records. Two local men looked suspicious. But one had a solid **alibi** for the night of the burglary.

The other suspect was a man named Lonnie Stout. Stout had been arrested several times for breaking and entering. One of these cases involved a restaurant. What's more, he lived less than a mile (1.6 km) from Burger Queen. And he had been known to walk around barefoot.

TOE NAILED
Are your toe prints unique?

Like your fingerprints, your toe prints are one-of-a-kind. A man named William Gourley learned that the hard way. In 1952, he was found guilty of trying to rob a bakery. The evidence? He had left a print of his left big toe at the scene.

That's not all. The ridges on the souls of your feet and the palms of your hands also form unique patterns. So just think of your hands and feet as permanent ID cards.

41

Busted Barefoot!

Police find a suspect. Will his feet match the prints?

The police drove to Lonnie Stout's house. They asked him where he had been the night of the burglary. Stout seemed nervous. Finally police asked if they could take a print impression of Stout's feet. Stout agreed and pulled off his shoes.

An officer rolled ink on Stout's feet. Stout then placed each foot on white paper. Police took the footprints back to the police department. There, they photographed the prints.

The police placed Stout's prints with the footprints from the crime. Then they sent the two sets of prints to the crime lab at the Tennessee Bureau of Investigation (TBI).

Agents at the crime lab compared the two samples. They were a perfect match.

Faced with the evidence, Stout confessed. He told police what had happened. During the burglary, he had not wanted to leave fingerprints at the scene. So he had used his socks to cover his hands!

Meanwhile, his bare feet left a trail of evidence! 24/7

THE EVIDENCE

26

ISO 64

THE CONCLUSION

The burglar had covered his hands with socks so he wouldn't leave fingerprints. But his footprints sent him to jail!

FORENSIC
DOWNLOAD

Here's even more amazing stuff about fingerprinting—right here at your fingertips.

1823 First Fingerprint Classification

In Europe, Johannes Purkinje created the first system for organizing fingerprints. His system divided all fingerprints into nine categories. People have been using fingerprints for identification for centuries. But Purkinje was the first to organize them.

1880 Don't Sweat It

A doctor from Scotland named Henry Faulds did a study on fingerprints. It was published in a magazine called *Nature*. What was his big discovery? Faulds discovered that sweat from fingerprints could be made visible with powders.

Key Dates in Fingerprinting

Fingerprints have left their own mark on history.

1883 Science Meets Police Work

French police official Alphonse Bertillon believed that no two people had exactly the same body measurements. He measured criminals' bodies. He used these numbers in a formula. His system, known as the Bertillon System, was used for a while to identify criminals.

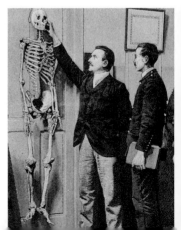

1896 Creating a Fingerprinting System

British official Sir Edward Henry developed a fingerprint system in 1896. The system divided prints into arches, loops, whorls, and composites. Henry's system became the basis of the system used in much of the world today.

1902 Prints Deliver Guilty Verdict

Harry Jackson stood in Central Criminal Court in London, charged with burglary. He pleaded not guilty. But police had found an imprint of his left thumb at the crime scene. During the trial, the jury saw blow-ups of this print and of one taken from Jackson. It was the first use of fingerprint evidence in a criminal trial. Jackson was found guilty—of stealing balls from a pool table!

1903 The Wild Will West Case

Will West arrived at Fort Leavenworth Prison in Kansas. The clerk took West's Bertillon measurements. Strangely enough, another prisoner named William West had exactly the same measurements. To make it more confusing, William West looked just like Will West!

How could they tell the two men apart? Officials found that the two men's fingerprints were nothing alike! The West case helped fingerprinting replace Bertillon as the leading tool for identification.

1990s AFIS Alert

The Automated Fingerprint Identification System (AFIS) was developed, making it a lot faster to find criminals. Law enforcement agencies use AFIS to search fingerprint databases around the country.

For more about AFIS, see page 23.

In the News

Fingerprints Help Free Man From Jail!

ROXBURY, MA— January 24, 2004

Stephan Cowans walked out of jail in Roxbury, Massachusetts, a free man. He had served six and one-half years for a crime a judge now says he didn't do.

Seven years ago, Cowans had been convicted of shooting a Boston police officer. However, a new look at a fingerprint proved Cowans was innocent. In the first trial, a fingerprint expert said that a print found on a glass at the scene was Cowans's. But new forensic testing proved that the "match was a mistake," said one official.

Stephan Cowans served almost seven years in jail for a crime officials now say he did not commit.

At Cowans's first trial, an expert said Cowans's prints were found at the crime scene. This was a huge mistake.

Looking for fingerprints on rocks used to be like looking for a needle in a haystack. Soon, fingerprints may be detected even on rocks!

New Spray Makes Fingerprints Stick

November 2003

Fingerprint experts have always stayed away from rough surfaces when they were dusting for prints. The best prints come from smooth surfaces. It's been impossible to get prints from rough surfaces, like bricks or stones. Until now, that is.

A new spray can help experts find fingerprints even on rough surfaces. Fingerprint expert Claude Roux says that now there's the "possibility that even rocks at outdoor crime scenes will yield valuable fingerprint evidence."

A new spray may make latent prints on rocks visible to the naked eye.

At Your Fingertips

See what kind of prints you're leaving. Then check out the tools and other stuff used by fingerprint specialists.

KINDS OF FINGERPRINTS

LOOP

There are three main categories of fingerprints. Which do you have? Have a look, but don't smudge them.

This is a **radial loop** on the thumb of someone's left hand. Radial loops open up on the opposite side from the second finger.

In **loop** fingerprints, the ridges form loops, one inside the other. See how the ridges go to the left, up, and down. That's the loop.

This is an **ulnar loop** on the thumb of someone's left hand. Ulnar loops open up on the side closest to the second finger.

Loops are the most common type of fingerprint. About 65% of people have loop fingerprints.

WHORL

About 30% of people have whorl fingerprints.

Here the loops form something called a **whorl**. As you can see, the ridges are in the shape of a circle.

This is a **central pocket** loop. It has a loop and a whorl right in the center.

The **double loop** has two loops.

This is an **accidental loop**. There's a whorl in the center.

ARCH

In **arch** fingerprints, the ridges form a single bump or wave. The ridges move up to form a little arch.

This a **tented arch** fingerprint. The arch makes a tent shape.

Arch fingerprints are pretty rare. Only about 5% of people have them.

TOOLS AND EQUIPMENT

powder, brush and tape Dusting is still the most popular way to find prints, so print specialists can't live without powder and a brush.

Super Glue Dusting isn't the only way to lift prints. Fumes from Super Glue make invisible prints visible, so they can be photographed. "Super Glue is one of the most valuable tools we have," says print specialist Oakley McKinney.

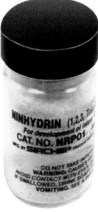

Ninhydrin Here's another way to lift prints. This chemical is used to get fingerprints from soft, absorbent surfaces like paper and clothing. The chemical reacts to acids in your skin, making prints show up. Ninhydrin can even develop prints made 30 years ago.

AFIS

AFIS (Automated Fingerprint Identification System) is a computer program that can search through several million prints on the computer in a few minutes.

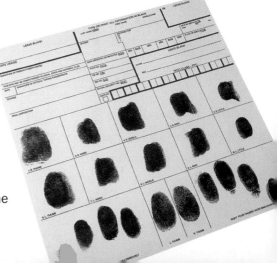

fingerprint ID card Here's the card used to record prints.

magnifier A comparison magnifier or magnifying glass is the print expert's best friend. Magnifying the print helps the examiner find all the unique details in the print.

gloves Fingerprint experts usually wear gloves. Why? They don't want to leave their own fingerprints around.

crime scope This tool uses UV light, which makes fingerprints glow. Presto!

FINDING A MATCH

Compare this AFIS print to the suspect's print.
A print specialist scanned the photo on the right into the AFIS system. The print on the left is the AFIS match.

HELP WANTED:
Fingerprint Analys

How'd you like to get your hands on a job as a fingerprint analyst? Here's more information about the field.

24/7: How did you become a latent print specialist?

AGENT MCKINNEY: I started my career with the FBI—that's where I got my fingerprint background. I eventually moved to the Tennessee Bureau of Investigation (TBI).

Oakley McKinney is a special agent with the TBI.

24/7: How would you become a print expert today?

AGENT MCKINNEY: Every law enforcement agency has different requirements. The TBI takes recent college graduates, who train for two years. We require that they have 24 hours of chemistry during college. And ideally, we'd like someone who studied forensics.

24/7: What's your typical day like?

AGENT MCKINNEY: My day varies greatly. Here, someone is always on call to go out to a crime scene. But most days I'm in the lab. I work on 25 to 30 cases at a time. Each one is at a different point in the investigation. On some cases, I'm waiting for photos. On others, I'm comparing photos and prints. I'm entering the prints into AFIS on other cases.

24/7: How is your job different from the crime scene investigators we see on TV?

AGENT MCKINNEY: On TV you'll see forensic specialists interviewing witnesses or suspects. That's pretty hokey. Our job is to collect, preserve, and examine the physical evidence that's left behind. It's not investigations.

24/7: What kinds of cases do print specialists work on?

AGENT MCKINNEY: Most cases overall are burglaries, but we work every crime — murder, rape, forgery, anything where a latent is available.

24/7: What do you like about your work?

AGENT MCKINNEY: I like figuring stuff out. I like working until I find and process a good print. It's kind of like a puzzle. And I like being part of a team that catches the bad guys.

24/7: What do you dislike?

AGENT MCKINNEY: To this day, I still don't like the blood and guts. But you just have to deal with it. You have to focus and be a professional and do your job.

Take this totally unscientific quiz to see if fingerprint analysis might be a good career for you.

1 **Do you stay away from gross stuff?**
a) No. In fact I'm really interested in how the body works.
b) I'm okay if it's not too gross.
c) I don't even like to see fake gross stuff on TV.

2 **Do you stick with a task even when it's hard?**
a) Yes, I never give up.
b) Sometimes, unless it's really boring.
c) No, when the going gets tough, I'm out of here.

3 **Do you enjoy working with computers?**
a) Definitely. I like how I can get lots of information.
b) Sometimes, but my eyes start to hurt after a while.
c) No. I never understand them.

4 **Are you concerned about justice?**
a) Yes, I want to make my area a safer place.
b) I like to watch crime shows on TV.
c) Someone else can do that.

5 **Are you good at spotting small details?**
a) Yes, I always notice everything.
b) I'm okay if I concentrate.
c) I just get the big picture.

YOUR SCORE

Give yourself 3 points for every "a" you chose. Give yourself 2 points for every "b" you chose. Give yourself 1 point for every "c" you chose.

If you got **13–15 points**, you'd probably be a good fingerprint analyst. If you got **10–12 points**, you might be a good fingerprint analyst. If you got **5–9 points**, you might want to look at another career!

1
2
3
4
5
6
7
8
9
10

INCHES

HOW TO GET STARTED...NOW!

It's never too early to start working toward your goals.

GET AN EDUCATION

▶ Starting now, take as many science courses as you can.

▶ Start thinking about college. Look for ones that have good forensics programs.

▶ Read the newspaper. Keep up with what's going on in your community.

▶ Read anything you can find about fingerprint analysis. See the books and Web sites in the Resources section on pages 56–58.

▶ Graduate from high school!

NETWORK!

Call your local law enforcement agency. Ask for the public affairs office. Find out if you can interview a print specialist about his or her job.

GET AN INTERNSHIP

Get an internship with a law enforcement agency—in the print lab, if possible.

LEARN ABOUT OTHER JOBS IN THE FIELD

▶ **Policing:** Police officers learn to work with investigative techniques, such as fingerprinting.

▶ **Information technology:** Agencies that conduct investigations need people with strong computer skills.

Resources

Looking for more information about forensic fingerprinting? Here are some resources you don't want to miss.

PROFESSIONAL ORGANIZATIONS

American Academy of Forensic Sciences (AAFS)
www.aafs.org
410 North 21st Street
Colorado Springs, CO 80904-2798
PHONE: 719-636-1100
FAX: 719-636-1993

The AAFS is an organization for forensic scientists. It helps them meet and share information with other forensic experts. Its Web site includes a long list of colleges and universities with forensic science programs.

Canadian Society of Forensic Science (CSFS)
www.csfs.ca
P.O. Box 37040
3332 McCarthy Road
Ottawa, Ontario
Canada K1V 0W0
PHONE: 613-738-0001
EMAIL: csfs@bellnet.ca

This nonprofit organization promotes the study of forensic science. Its Web site has information about careers and schools with forensic science programs.

International Association for Identification (IAI)
www.theiai.org
2535 Pilot Knob Road, Suite 117
Mendota Heights, MN 55120-1120

CLPE means Certified Latent Print Examiner. Fingerprint examiners who have these letters beside their names have been certified by the IAI. IAI-certified print examiners have passed tests that prove they have top-notch skills. Its Web site includes job listings and requirements.

EDUCATION AND TRAINING

The AAFS Web site **(www.aafs.org)** has a list of colleges and universities with forensic science programs.

Federal Bureau of Investigation (FBI)
www.fbi.gov/
J. Edgar Hoover Building
935 Pennsylvania Avenue, NW
Washington, DC 20535-0001
PHONE: 210-567-3177
EMAIL: smile@uthscsa.edu

The FBI Web site contains information on its latent print unit. It also gives information on getting a job with the FBI.

WEB SITES

Court TV's Crime Library
www.crimelibrary.com/index.html
This Web site contains tons of true criminal cases. There's a whole section on fingerprinting.

Fingerprint Dictionary
www.fprints.nwlean.net
A long list of terms used by fingerprint experts.

The Fingerprint Society
www.fpsociety.org.uk
News and a journal from fingerprint buffs in England.

Latent Print Examination
www.onin.com/fp
There's good info on this site for professionals and for the general public.

Southern California Association of Fingerprint Officers (SCAFO)
www.scafo.org
The Web site for this organization lists job information and useful links.

BOOKS FOR KIDS ABOUT FORENSIC SCIENCE

Fingerprinting (Great Explorations in Math and Science). Berkeley: University of California, 2000.

Innes, Brian. *The Search for Forensic Evidence.* Milwaukee: Gareth Stevens Publishing, 2005.

Mauro, Paul, and Robin Epstein. *Prints and Impressions.* New York: Scholastic, 2003.

Platt, Richard. *Forensics.* Boston: Kingfisher, 2005.

Silverstein, Herma. *Threads of Evidence: Using Forensic Science to Solve Crimes.* New York: Henry Holt & Company, 1996.

Just for fun, check out these classic novels. Twain wrote about fingerprinting before fingerprinting was cool!

Life on the Mississippi by Mark Twain

Pudd'nhead Wilson by Mark Twain

A

absorbent (ab-ZOR-buhnt) *adjective* able to soak up water or other liquid

AFIS (AY-fiss) *noun* a computer database in which police store the prints of arrested suspects. AFIS stands for *Automated Fingerprint Identification System.*

alibi (AL-uh-bye) *noun* a story about where you were when something happened

analyst (AN-ah-list) *noun* someone who is specially trained in studying something

arch (arch) *noun* a fingerprint pattern that is made up of a single raised bump or wave. A **tented arch** fingerprint has a tent shape.

B

busted (BUS-tid) *verb* slang for *caught*

C

carbon paper (CAR-bun pay-pur) *noun* paper containing carbon ink on one side for making copies. It was used with typewriters before computers and copiers were common.

D

dactylography (dac-ti-LOG-rah-fee) *noun* the study of fingerprints as a method of identification

database (DAY-tuh-bayss) *noun* a lot of information organized on a computer

DNA (DEE-en-ay) *noun* stuff in almost every cell of your body that has tons of information about you

duct (duhkt) *noun* a passage that allows air to move around in a building

dusted (DUS-ted) *verb* brushed with a dark powder on a surface at a crime scene. The dust sticks to the sweat and oils in the latent prints, which makes invisible prints visible!

E

evidence (EV-uh-duhnss) *noun* information or clues that might help solve a crime

expert (EX-purt) *noun* someone who has special knowledge or training in a given subject. See page 12 for some forensic experts.

F

FBI (EF-bee-eye) *noun* a U.S. government agency that investigates major crimes. It stands for *Federal Bureau of Investigation*.

fingerprint (FIN-ger-print) *noun* the pattern of skin ridges at the tips of your finger. These patterns include arches, loops, and whorls.

forensic (FOR-en-ziks) *adjective* describing a science used to help investigate or solve crimes

fuming (FEW-ming) *verb* a process that makes latent prints visible

G

groove (groov) *noun* the area between the ridges of your fingerprint

H

hit (hit) *noun* a match. A hit on AFIS means the computer found a match.

I

identify (eye-DEN-tuh-fye) *verb* to figure out who someone is

impressed print (im-PRESD print) *noun* a print made when you touch something like gum, which leaves a clear impression

J

jury (JU-ree) *noun* a group of people at trial who listen to a case and decide if a person is guilty or innocent

L

latent print (LAY-tuhnt print) *noun* a fingerprint or footprint that you can't see. When you touch stuff, the sweat and oils on your skin leave a mark. That means that every time you touch a hard, shiny surface, you're leaving an invisible fingerprint.

lift (lift) *verb* to pick up a fingerprint, using sticky tape

loop (loop) *noun* a fingerprint pattern in which the ridges form a series of half-circles, one inside the other. There are **accidental**, **central pocket**, **double**, **radial**, and **ulnar loop** fingerprints.

N

Ninhydrin (NIN-hy-drihn) *noun* a chemical used to get fingerprints from soft, absorbent surfaces like paper and clothing

P

partial (PAR-shul) *noun* part of a fingerprint

patent print (PAT-uhnt print) *noun* a print that is clearly visible. It's made when you touch something like paint or blood and then touch other surfaces.

perp (purp) *noun* slang for *perpetrator*, one who commits a crime

process (PRAH-ses) *verb* to gather information (such as fingerprint evidence) at a crime scene

prints (prints) *noun* short for *fingerprints*

R

ridges (RI-jez) *noun* raised lines on the tips of your finger that create your fingerprint. The area between the ridges is called a groove.

S

specialist (SPEH-shul-ist) *noun* someone who knows a lot about a particular subject

suspect (SUS-pekt) *noun* a person the police think might be guilty of a crime

T

trace evidence (trayss EV-uh-duhnss) *noun* fibers, tire tracks, shoe prints, and other stuff left behind at the scene of the crime and used to help catch the criminal

W

whorl (whirl) *noun* a fingerprint pattern in which the ridges form a series of circles, one inside the other

Index

Author's Note

When I started researching this book, all I knew about fingerprinting was what I saw on TV crime shows. But as latent print specialist Oakley McKinney told me, "The TV shows make it look like magic. But it's really science."

I learned tons about the history and science of fingerprinting. I learned so much I couldn't fit it all in this book. I started with Web sites. So if you're into finding out more, hop on your computer. Check out the Web sites listed in the Resources section. If you like reading about cases, try the Court TV site. The IAI and FBI Web sites give valuable info on getting a job in the field.

There are textbooks on fingerprinting that really show how to compare prints. You can find them at large bookstores. They zero in on the details of what experts look for. But they're pretty complex, so have your dictionary handy!

Of course, the best way to learn is to talk to those who do it. I contacted the public relations/public affairs departments of the FBI and TBI. The PR person put me in touch with Agent McKinney. So try calling your local law enforcement office—the police or sheriff's department—and ask for the public information officer or the public relations person. Find out if you can interview a print specialist about his or her job. It won't hurt to try!

Here's to catching the bad guys!

ACKNOWLEDGMENTS

I would like to thank Agent Oakley McKinney for teaching me the nitty gritty about fingerprint analysis. Thanks also to the TBI for their cooperation, and to the American Academy of Forensic Sciences.

CONTENT ADVISER: King C. Brown, MS, CSCSA, CFPH, CLPE, Crime Scene Supervisor, West Palm Beach (Flordia) Police Department